Business Planning Workbook

2019/20 edition

(enter your name)

....

trading as

(enter business trading name)

....

Written by John McGaughran, Director
Training for Employment (Yorkshire) CIC
https://www.trainingforemployment.co.uk/

© Copyright 2013-2019 Training for Employment (Yorkshire) CIC
All rights reserved

BUSINESS PLANNING WORKBOOK

INDEX

Index..	Page 2
Introduction and example: Cyril's Cycle Centre..........	Page 3
Executive Summary..	Pages 4 & 5
Personal / Management Details	Pages 6 & 7
Personal Survival Budget...	Page 8
Start-up Costs..	Page 9
SWOT Analysis..	Pages 10 & 11
Market Segmentation...	Pages 12 & 13
Marketing Plan..	Pages 14 & 15
Legal and Administration...	Pages 16 & 17
Financial Information..	Page 18
Premises...	Page 19
Funding...	Page 20 & 21
Forecast Profit and Loss...	Page 22
Financial Analysis..	Page 23
Cashflow Forecast...	Page 24
Conclusion	Page 25
Legislation Which Affects Most Businesses..............	Page 26
Useful Websites	Page 27

Version 04.19

About the author

John McGaughran is a Fellow of the Institute of Enterprise and Entrepreneurs (IOEE) and holds a Level 7 in Business Improvement and Contract Management. He is a qualified tutor in the lifelong learning sector, holding a Level 3 in Education & Training. John has previously run other businesses as a sole trader and as a Member in a Partnership, and is currently Director of Training for Employment (Yorkshire) C.I.C., a not-for-profit Community Interest Company.

Introduction

"Failing to plan is planning to fail!" - *attributed to Alan Lakein*

Your **Business Plan** forms a solid foundation on which to build your business. It is a written document that describes a business, its objectives, its strategies, the market it is in and its financial forecasts. It has a number of functions, from securing external funding to measuring success within your business. Ultimately, writing your **Business Plan** will help ensure that you have thought things through thoroughly and so maximise the chances of your business succeeding rather than faltering and, perhaps, ultimately failing.

This workbook aims to help you understand the basic issues around starting a business. It will help you identify both personal and business needs and provide you with the knowledge and understanding necessary to develop your **Business Plan**. This will give you and your business every chance of meeting future opportunities and overcoming challenges.

To help you to understand some aspects of writing a **Business Plan**, we shall be using a case study based on a fictional business - *Cyril's Cycle Centre.*

PLEASE NOTE – in general, throughout this workbook, you will find instructions and examples on the left-hand page. You will find the pages that will form your **Business Plan** on the right-hand side.

Anything written in **this colour** is instructional or is an example.

Whenever the workbook refers to a 'Product', it can also be read as a 'Service'.

By the time you have completed this Business Planning Workbook, you will have a good overview of the knowledge and skills required to become self-employed, or to start up a small business.

Good luck with your venture!

Executive Summary – How to write a First Draft

This is a one page summary of your Business Plan. Imagine that someone doesn't have the time to read your whole Business Plan in detail, but needs to get a good feel for your business and plans. This page will help others understand your business idea. Think Dragon's Den!

This page would normally be the last page you complete, but it may be useful to create an initial outline now, to capture your initial thoughts and ideas. Let's have a look at *Cyril's* Executive Summary (first draft), which should include the following:

- **Idea Summary:** A short phrase which describes your legal status, main business activity, intended customers and intended place of business.

    e.g. A sole trader set up to sell high quality cycles, parts and accessories, and to service cycles of all types, for cycling enthusiasts throughout Yorkshire.

- **Mission Statement:** A short, 'punchy' statement describing what your business does and the benefits it brings to its customers.

    e.g. Cyril's Cycle Centre is a one-stop shop for all your cycling needs, inspiring healthier transport for a fitter, healthier tomorrow.

- **Outline Market:** A general description of the market for your products and / or services, i.e. who your potential customers will be.

    e.g. The main market for services will be cycle enthusiasts and anyone interested in starting cycling as a sport or for leisure.

- **Operation Outline:** A short phrase to describe how the business will operate, how the product or services will be supplied to customers, and type of premises.

    e.g. The business will be run from a high street premises, with a showroom and an on-site workshop. A range of cycles and accessories will be displayed in the showroom. Customers looking for repairs or improvements to their current cycle will be offered a quotation after a thorough inspection. Any agreed work will be arranged at a time to suit the customer and will be carried out on the premises.

- **Financial Summary:** A short paragraph outlining the sales you hope to achieve, the prices you are likely to charge, and how you will fund your business.

    e.g. Prices will vary, depending upon the choice of bicycle or the complexity of the repair or upgrade to an existing bicycle. To start the business, £30,000 is being sought from the bank, with the owner also investing £30,000.
    Turnover is forecast at £33,000 in the first year, producing a net profit of £21,000 before tax.

EXECUTIVE SUMMARY

Idea summary:

Mission statement:

Outline market:

Operation outline:

Financial summary:

Management Details – this is all about you!

The Management Details section is your chance to tell anyone reading your Business Plan about any qualifications and experience which are relevant to the business or industry that you are in. This is also useful to reassure yourself - and any potential funders - that you are the right person running your business and have the skills, expertise and experience required. Funders and supporters will not want to risk time and money on a business that is beyond the capabilities of the person running it.

Legal Trading Status - e.g. Sole Trader, Limited Company; see page 16 for more details.

Qualifications are only important as long as they are relevant. Any qualification tells the reader of your Business Plan that you are qualified, capable of hard work and resilient. Specifically, a recent NVQ in the subject of your business would carry more weight than, for example, a decades-old GCSE!

Your experience does not have to come just from your past employment. For example, someone who has worked as a joiner for 20 years may not seem to have the skills to start a church interior restoration programme. However, if they have spent many years restoring furniture and have worked on period furniture in particular, then those joinery skills *are* likely to be transferable.

In the same way as your Executive Summary gives a clear and easy to understand summary of your Business Plan, the Personal Profile section gives a clear and easy to understand summary of you. It creates a positive first impression of you and the benefits you will bring to your business.

Let's have a look at Cyril's qualifications:

NVQ in Customer Service.
A-Level Maths, English and Business Studies

Cyril's experience:

Twelve years experience working as an employee in the cycle department of a retail store, serving customers, repairing bikes, giving advice on correct parts, etc. Stock control and cashing up.

Cyril's personal profile:

Mr Cyril Sykes has enjoyed cycling from an early age and learned cycle maintenance in his teens. This led to a hobby in repairing and maintaining his friends' bicycles. On leaving college, Mr Sykes obtained a job in the cycle department of a large retail store. He works well with others, motivating and encouraging them. He is energetic, physically fit and technically competent. Cyril identifies and develops opportunities, enjoys a challenge and, after twelve years as an employee, has decided to start his own business.

Notice, the profile has been written in the third person, i.e. no 'I am' statements. This makes it sound like someone else is describing Cyril in this way, and so the information has more impact.

PERSONAL / MANAGEMENT DETAILS

Name	
Address	
Post Code	
Telephone	
E-mail	
Website Address	
Social Media	

Legal Trading Status (e.g. Sole Trader)

Qualifications: (Relevant to Business idea)

Experience: (Relevant to Business idea)

Personal Profile: (Written in the 'third person')

PERSONAL SURVIVAL BUDGET

This is a calculation to help you understand what profit you need from your business in order for you to keep your current lifestyle when your business starts.

(A) ESTIMATED EXPENDITURE (by you and your family)
To enable you to survive the **next 12 months**

Mortgage / Rent	£	Car (Personal Use)	£
Council Tax	£	Home Repairs / Decorating / Garden	£
Water Usage / Rates	£	Haircuts / Styling	£
Gas / Electricity	£	Children's Expenses	£
Food & Housekeeping	£	Hire Charges / Credit Cards	£
Property/Personal Insurance	£	Savings	£
Pension/ Investment Contributions	£	Subscriptions (Clubs, etc.)	£
Clothing / Footwear	£	Entertainment / Hobbies	£
Telephone / Internet (Personal Use)	£	Costs if living with Parent/Guardian	£
TV Licence / Subscriptions	£	Contingencies (around 10%)	£
		TOTAL (A)	£

(B) ESTIMATED **ANNUAL** PERSONAL INCOME from family/partner/investments/pension/other sources – NOT your business.
(include means-tested Benefits such as Housing Allowance, Council Tax Support, Working / Child Tax Credits, Universal Credit or ESA).

	£
	£
	£
TOTAL (B)	£

SURVIVAL INCOME REQUIRED from your BUSINESS (Total A minus Total B)	£

BUSINESS START UP COSTS

This is a calculation to help you understand how much you will need to invest in your business before you can commence trading. Any costs which have been incurred up to six months prior to starting up, can be set against your profits. Keep all receipts!

Required? (✓)		Cost £	
	Premises		
	Property Purchase		
	Rent in advance (usually 1 month)		
	Business Rates		
	Installation costs and/or advance payment for Electricity		
	Installation costs and/or advance payment for Gas		
	Installation costs and/or advance payment for Water		
	Insurance - buildings and/or contents		
	Telephone - landline installation and advance rental		
	Property refurbishment incl. painting & decorating		
	Fire and Safety Equipment		
		subtotal:	£
	Insurance (consider a discount for trade association membership)		
	Public Liability (annual premium based on £1m - £5m cover)		
	Product Liability Insurance		
	Professional Indemnity Insurance		
	Employers Liability Insurance		
		subtotal:	£
	Stationery, Advertising and Branding Costs		
	Business Cards		
	Letterheads / Compliments Slips		
	Advertising Flyers / Posters		
	Advertisements, e.g. local newspapers		
	Website		
	Signwriting, e.g. shop front, vehicle		
		subtotal:	£
	Transport costs		
	Road Tax (if due imminently)		
	Vehicle Insurance (include Class 1 Business use)		
	Vehicle purchase - if required to start up		
		subtotal:	£
	Professional Services and Licences		
	Accountant / Bookkeeper (if required)		
	Solicitor, e.g. for setting up a property leasehold agreement		
	Food Hygiene Licence		
	Health and Safety Certificate		
	CRB / DBS (Criminal Record Check)		
		subtotal:	£
	Contingencies (around 20%)	subtotal:	£
	Initial Stock / Equipment / Furniture required to start		
	1)		
	2)		
		subtotal:	£
	TOTAL REQUIREMENT to start up		£

© 2013-2019 Training for Employment (Yorkshire) C.I.C. All rights reserved.

SWOT ANALYSIS (Strengths, Weaknesses, Opportunities, Threats)

A SWOT analysis is a framework that can be used for assessing your personal attributes, competition, customers and markets.
It is useful to complete the SWOT with someone who knows you and your business idea.

S — Strengths
Your positive personal attributes and selling points. You have some control over these.

W — Weaknesses
Your internal negative attributes. You have some control over these as well.

O — Opportunities
Uncontrollable external events that you can potentially take advantage of.

T — Threats
Uncontrollable external factors that may work against you and require you to take protective action.

Example SWOT Analysis — *Cyril's Cycle Centre*

Strengths	Weaknesses
- 12 years experience bicycle retail industry - £60,000 capital investment - City & Guilds Certificate in Customer Service - Only direct bike parts seller in local area - Solid network of contacts within the industry - Enthusiastic off-road cyclist - Secretary to local cycling club	- Just starting up in business - Unfamiliar with modern accounting - Manual book-keeping - Limited IT skills - Weak on marketing skills
Opportunities	**Threats**
- Chance to write regular articles for local press - Renewed public interest in cycling with Olympics in 2012 and Tour de France in 2014, the Tour de Yorkshire in 2015&17, and the UCI World Championships 2019. - An opportunity to promote more environmentally friendly transport and leisure activity - To provide a one-stop shop for all cycling needs - Online ordering facilities for products not stocked	- Cycling has suddenly become popular, so more competition is likely - If owner becomes ill, or cannot work, they will need to pay for temporary staff - Keeping up with new trends in cycling could become prohibitively expensive - Economic and general threats (e.g., recession) - Competition from internet sales

BUSINESS SWOT ANALYSIS

STRENGTHS	**W**EAKNESSES
OPPORTUNITIES	**T**HREATS

Also consider **PEST** which stands for **P**olitical, **E**conomic, **S**ociological, **T**echnological; and **PESTLE**, which adds **L**egal and **E**nvironmental factors.

Market Segmentation

Market segmentation is one of the steps that goes into defining and targeting specific markets. It is the process of dividing a market into distinct groups of buyers that require different products or different marketing approaches. This process is sometimes referred to as 'customer groups'.

As customers have different needs and wants, it would be impossible for businesses to try to adapt their products and services for each individual customer. It is much more cost effective for businesses today to aim at selling to a particular group (or groups) of customers, i.e. a specific market segment.

The more information and statistics you have about a target market, the more precise you can be in developing your marketing strategy. When you identify market segments, you will find it easier and more effective to develop marketing approaches to satisfy your customers' needs.

Your business must analyse the needs and wants of different market segments (customer groups) before determining its own niche market. To be effective in market segmentation, consider the following:

- Segments or target markets should be accessible to the business

- Each segmented group must be large enough to provide a profitable customer base

- Each segmented group may require a separate marketing plan

There are many reasons for dividing your market into smaller segments. Any time you suspect that there are significant, measurable differences in your market, you should consider market segmentation. By doing so, you will make marketing easier, discover niche markets and become more efficient with your marketing resources.

There are a variety of ways in which you can segment your market, including the following segments:

- **Demographic**   e.g. age, race, gender, nationality, occupation, income (Type)
- **Psychographic** e.g. lifestyle, motives and personality (Psychology)
- **Geographic**   e.g. where your customers live or do business (Location)
- **Behavioural**   e.g. recreation habits, leisure activities, travel (Habits)
- **Lifestyle**   e.g. health, luxury, environmental concerns (Goals)

A practical example of market segmentation: Cyril knows that one part of his demographic target market is retired adults who enjoy keeping fit (i.e. demographic and behavioural segments), and are frequent buyers of and sports equipment. Cyril can create an advertising message to appeal directly to those buyers. He could also offer discounts to them on a day that is usually less busy, in order to attract additional custom on that day (e.g. early or midweek).

When writing your marketing flyers, or any other promotional material, including press releases, keep in mind the idea of market segmentation or customer group. Tailor your marketing message to that group, or those groups, with whom you wish to communicate.

Remember – make it easy for your chosen market to part with their money!

The Marketing Mix - the four P's

The marketing mix was first coined by Neil Borden, the president of the American Marketing Association, in 1953. It defines the four **P**'s of marketing and promotion. They are **P**roduct, **P**rice, **P**romotion and **P**lace. They will all have a bearing on your target market and potential business success. Make a mistake with one and it could seriously affect the future of your business venture.

Product (or Service):
Marketers should consider how to:
- make best use of resources
- position the product relative to competitors
- exploit their brand
- exploit the company's resources
- configure the product mix so that each product complements the other.

The marketer must also consider product development strategies (e.g. the improvement of products / services, and the creation of new ones.

Place: Refers to providing the product at a place which is convenient for consumers to access.
This can be a physical place, such as a premises, or via the internet. Think of 'place' as the distribution channel - how the product reaches the customer.

Price:
There are two main types of pricing to consider

- **Cost plus pricing**; The cost of your goods / services *plus* overheads, *plus* the amount you need to make a profit.

- **Value based pricing**; The price you believe your customers are prepared to pay. Their perceived *value*.

Promotion: This is the method(s) used to **market** your product or service. This consists of direct advertising, internet advertising, and the company's own website.

It also includes **Public Relations**, which consists of press releases, sponsorship, exhibitions and trade fairs, customer and industry product reviews, press articles, etc.

MARKETING PLAN

PRODUCTS OR SERVICES TO BE SOLD

A brief outline of the products and / or services you plan to sell, from detail on page 4 of Business Plan template, or from page 5 of workbook.

Make your summary interesting and 'punchy'.

Include a description of the main features of your offering, and the benefits which these features will give your potential customers or clients.

WHO WILL YOUR MAJOR CUSTOMERS BE?

Having identified your potential market from research carried out, describe your target market.
Include market segmentation, as described on page 12.

WHAT MARKET RESEARCH HAVE YOU CARRIED OUT?

Have you identified, and spoken to potential customers?
Have you commissioned surveys?
Given free samples of your product / service to a group of testers?
Have you looked at current market research, reports, etc.?
What conclusions did you make from this research?
Is there a large enough group of passionate, interested buyers for your offering?

WHAT PROMOTIONAL ACTIVITY WILL YOU CARRY OUT?

For example, using press releases, social media.

In all your marketing, promotions and communications, make sure you sell the benefits of your product / service to your customers.

COMPETITORS – Who might they be?

List up to three of your main competitors, plus their locations.

COMPETITORS' MAIN STRENGTHS AND WEAKNESSES

Refer to your SWOT Analysis, page 11.

Strengths:

Weaknesses:

YOUR MAIN STRENGTHS AND WEAKNESSES

Again, refer to your SWOT Analysis.

Strengths:

Weaknesses:

BASIS OF PRICING

For example, do you charge an hourly rate, or a day rate, and what is this rate £?

The following calculation will determine the minimum hourly rate which you will need to charge to cover the living expenses on your Survival Budget on page 8:
(Annual Personal Survival Budget £............+ All Annual Business Overheads £..........)
÷ Annual Hours worked.......... = Hourly Rate required £..........

MAJOR SUPPLIERS (if applicable)

Who are they? (List their names, what they supply, and their locations)

YOUR BUSINESS OBJECTIVES IN THE NEXT 1, 3 and 5 YEARS

Objectives should be '**SMART**'.
State how your objectives are **S**pecific, **M**easurable, **A**chievable, **R**ealistic, and have a **T**imescale in which they can be achieved?

Legal and Administration - Types of Business Structure

The description of 'self-employed' applies to many types of , including farmers, taxi and cab drivers, those running their own businesses, freelancers and contractors.

There are nine main types of entity for the self-employed to consider:
- Sole Trader (unincorporated)
- Partnership (unincorporated)
- Limited Company (Ltd.)
- Limited Liability Partnership (LLP)
- Social Enterprise (unincorporated)
- Community Interest Company (C.I.C.)
- Charity or Charitable Trust
- Constituted Sports Club
- Community Amateur Sports Club (CASC)

Setting up as a Sole Trader

Becoming a sole trader is the simplest way to get your new business off the ground. Once you have told HMRC of your intention to become self employed, you can start trading immediately (subject to any industry-specific licenses you might need).

Sole traders can adapt quickly to any changes in their businesses, without having to concern themselves with a great deal of bureaucracy. As a sole trader, you will have complete control over your business and finances.

However, as no distinction is made between your personal and business finances, you will be ultimately liable should anything go wrong. For this reason, it is worth spending time considering which business structure is best for you.

Setting up as an 'incorporated' business

Sole traders and simple partnerships only need inform HMRC. However, Limited Companies, Limited Liability Partnerships and the other legal entities above, also need to notify CompaniesHouse.gov.uk, and have additional administrative, accounting and reporting requirements. Charities must report to the CharityCommission.gov.uk

A Not For Profit (also called a Social Enterprise) is a general term to describe the way a business operates for the good of the community. A Community Interest Company (CIC) is much the same as a Limited Company, but a CIC is set up with the aim of reinvesting surplus profit towards the 'social aims' of the Company, instead of those profits being for the benefit of the owners, Directors and/or shareholders.

So, a CIC offers the same protections as a Ltd Company, but provides a gateway for funding, because it's legal structure sets out in binding terms, the social aims of the Company.

If you are unsure whether or not you need to register as self-employed, you can refer to the leaflet 'Employed or Self Employed' for Tax & National Insurance from the HMRC website.

LEGAL AND ADMINISTRATION

TRADING STATUS
e.g. Sole Trader, Partnership, Limited Company, Community Interest Company, Charity. State your reasons for choosing this type of trading entity.

WHAT ARE THE STATUTORY AND LOCAL REQUIREMENTS FOR THE CHOSEN OPTION? (Include any Permits, Licences, Insurances etc)
HMRC says 'Register as soon as you can after starting your business. At the latest, you should register by 5 October in your business's second tax year.' This means that you must register at the very latest by 5th October 2020, which is after the end of the *current* tax year, which will be 5th April 2020. If you do not register, you could incur a penalty.

FINANCE REQUIRED
Do you require any finance to get started? If so, what is the source, e.g. your own funds, friends/family, a bank loan, etc. Also state how much money is required and for what purpose. State the name of your business bank.

START-UP SCHEDULE		
Timetable of actions to be taken to be ready for Trading, e.g. marketing	By when? e.g. date or month	Cost £

FINANCIAL INFORMATION

WHAT SYSTEM OF ACCOUNTS DO YOU PROPOSE TO USE?
🏐 For example, Manual Cash-book, Computer Spreadsheet, or software. 🏐 Personal Tax Accounts now online. Making Tax Digital is due in 2019 for businesses with a turnover above the VAT threshold. 🏐 The 'Open Banking' protocol should enable efficient financial control. 🏐 Please note, you are obliged - by law - to retain your business records for at least <u>six</u> years; e.g. accounts from April 2019 will need to be retained until 1st May 2025.

HOW WILL YOU MONITOR THE FINANCIAL PROGRESS OF THE BUSINESS?
🏐 Monitor income and outgoings against the Cashflow Forecast, on a monthly basis 🏐 Take any remedial action necessary to keep on track.

WHAT PROVISION HAVE YOU MADE FOR TAX?
🏐 After the annual Personal Allowance of £12,500, you can put aside 25% of additional profits into a separate savings account on a regular basis ready for the first Self Assessment 'Tax Bill' payment. Class 2 National Insurance (NI) Contributions are currently £3.00 per week. The annual 'Small Profits Threshold' is £6,365. 🏐 Class 4 National Insurance is payable at 9% on annual profits of between £8,632 and £50,000 (after which you will pay 2%). 🏐 Class 2 and Class 4 NI are now paid directly in Self-Assessment payment. 🏐 'I will monitor the tax thresholds, which are likely to change on an annual basis with each Government Budget.' If in doubt, check with HMRC.

WILL YOU REQUIRE TO REGISTER FOR V.A.T. – if so, when?
The current threshold for having to register for V.A.T. stands at an annual turnover of £85,000. This threshold will probably change on an annual basis. 'Making Tax Digital' is due in 2019 (for V.A.T. only) 'I will monitor my income on a three monthly basis and will register for VAT if and when it becomes necessary, i.e. if it appears that my turnover will exceed £85,000'

RISK ANALYSIS
🏐 If your business fails, what are the financial consequences for your and your family? 🏐 What is the 'worst-case scenario'? 🏐 Can the risk be mitigated, e.g. by taking out insurance; or by taking on a business partner?

PREMISES

LOCATION	*If working from home*, please tick here ☐ Otherwise, state the address and postcode of your proposed working premises.

Floor Area (m²)		Purchase Cost	
Term of Lease		Period Outstanding	
Present Rent		Next Rent Review Due	
Alteration Costs		Planning Permission	
Building Regulations		Planning Authority	

EQUIPMENT

Existing Equipment		£
		£
	Total Existing Equipment	£

Proposed Equipment		£
		£
		£
		£
	Total Proposed Equipment	£

VEHICLES

EXISTING		£
PROPOSED		£

Funding Required

When starting a new business, you will need to thoroughly research your new venture so that you can demonstrate to yourself, as well as to any potential lender or investor, that there is a need for your product or service.

Instead of going elsewhere for your finance, could you start building your business on a smaller scale, funding it yourself in the early stages? Could you freelance, or work part-time, whilst your business gets off the ground?

Funding could come from friends and family, or from a loan from a bank or finance company, or from crowd-funding. Can you access grant funding? Or match funded schemes?

Things you may need to fund include:

Equipment: Equipment you already own should be listed under **'Existing Equipment'** (on page 12 of the Business Plan). Any equipment you may require to start the business, e.g. tools, computers, printers, vehicles, etc. should be listed under **'Proposed Equipment'** on the same page of the Business Plan. In each case, state their cost or current market value.

Purchasing equipment, by taking finance, will add commitments and overheads to your business. Think about cash flow and consider all options before committing yourself to unnecessary overheads.

- Could you lease equipment instead, e.g. a van or a computer system?
- Can you hire machinery, e.g. rent a rotavator rather than buy one?
- What is the most tax efficient option for you and your business?

Premises: The first question you need to ask yourself is, 'Do I really need premises?'

If the answer is 'Yes' and you are going to rent premises, you may need to purchase a lease and you will need to engage a solicitor. Leasing can be expensive, with the money often required in advance. You may also need to do work on the building before you start trading, including installing telephone, power and water connections, refurbishment and signage.

You need to consider change of use planning permission, etc. These costs will add to the investment you need to start the business.

If you are working from home, you may need to get an additional phone line installed, or office furniture, etc., perhaps in a spare bedroom.

If you have already spent money in making premises ready in anticipation of starting your business, this needs to show as **'Capital Introduced'** in your accounts. It must also be shown as **'Own Cash'** in the Summary of Funding Sources (on page 13 of the Business Plan).

When your business can afford to repay the **'Capital Introduced'**, show this as **'Capital Repaid'** in your accounts.

Working Capital: There are other things you will need to pay for before any money comes into the business. They can include buying materials, stock, advertising, business stationery and your 'Own Drawings' (the technical term for your personal wage as a business owner). You are likely to have to pay for these before you have made any sales or received money from the sales you have made. The amount of money you need to pay for these expenses is called Working Capital.

FUNDING

SUMMARY OF CAPITAL COSTS

PREMISES	Purchase	£
	First Month's Rent	£
	Lease Premium (if applicable)	£
	Alterations	£
	Fixtures and Fittings	£

PROPOSED STOCK, MACHINERY OR PLANT (From page 19 Proposed Equipment)		£
VEHICLES		£
WORKING CAPITAL (And / or excess capital from Funding)		£
	TOTAL (Must match total below)	£

SUMMARY OF FUNDING SOURCES (page 10 of Business Plan)

OWN CASH		£
BANK LOAN		£
BANK OVERDRAFT		£
OTHER GRANTS (Please specify)		£
OTHER (Please specify)		£
	TOTAL (Must match total above)	£

FORECAST PROFIT & LOSS ACCOUNT
FOR THE CURRENT TAX YEAR
(Figures can be taken from example Cashflow Forecast on p.24)

TOTAL SALES INCOME (A)		£
LESS VARIABLE COSTS (B) (or 'Cost of Sales')	£	
GROSS PROFIT (C) This is Total Sales (A) less Variable Costs (B)		£
LESS OVERHEADS		
RENT & RATES	£	
INSURANCE	£	
POSTAGE & PACKING	£	
ROAD TAX	£	
VEHICLE COSTS	£	
ADVERTISING	£	
TRAVEL EXPENSES	£	
STATIONERY	£	
SIGNAGE / SHOPFRONT	£	
WEBSITE	£	
TELEPHONE	£	
REPAIRS AND RENEWALS	£	
HEAT & LIGHT	£	
SUNDRIES	£	
PROFESSIONAL FEES	£	
TOTAL OVERHEADS (D)	£	
	NET PROFIT FOR YEAR This is Gross Profit (C) minus Total Overheads (D) <u>before</u> own drawings and tax	£

FINANCIAL ANALYSIS FROM YOUR FORECAST PROFIT & LOSS ACCOUNT

FOR THE CURRENT YEAR

(Figures taken from Profit & Loss on page 22)

The following figures analyse the profit margin, amount of sales required to break even, and the number of weeks this will take to happen.

However, the results from the calculations are spread over the entire 12-month period.

N.B. All figures are before Tax, National Insurance Class 4 and Own Drawings.

The figures in the purple sections (............) are taken from the Cashflow on p.24, or from the Profit & Loss p.22

GROSS PROFIT MARGIN

$$\frac{\text{GROSS PROFIT } £ \text{............}}{\text{TOTAL SALES } £ \text{............}} = \text{............} \times 100 = \text{.......} \%$$

BREAK EVEN SALES

$$\frac{\text{TOTAL OVERHEADS } £ \text{............}}{\text{GROSS PROFIT MARGIN .... \%}} = \text{............} \times 100 = £ \text{............}$$

NUMBER OF WEEKS IN WHICH BREAK EVEN SALES WILL BE ACHIEVED

$$\frac{\text{BREAK EVEN SALES } £ \text{............}}{\text{TOTAL SALES } £ \text{............}} = \text{............} \times 52 = \text{......} \text{ Weeks}$$

CASHFLOW FORECAST

	Month 1 Budget March	Month 2 Budget April	Month 3 Budget May	Month 4 Budget June	Month 5 Budget July	Month 6 Budget August	Month 7 Budget September	Month 8 Budget October	Month 9 Budget November	Month 10 Budget December	Month 11 Budget January	Month 12 Budget February	Year Budget
SALES													
1 Touring Bikes	318	636	1,113	1,590	1,590	1,590	1,590	795	0	795	0	159	10,176
2 Mountain Bike	1,495	2,093	2,691	2,990	3,588	3,588	2,990	2,990	1,495	2,392	299	598	27,209
3 Kona Process Touring Bikes	0	0	1,200	1,200	2,400	2,400	1,200	1,200	0	0	0	0	9,600
4 Parts and Accessories	100	100	250	350	600	600	350	200	0	750	0	0	3,300
5 TOTAL SALES	1,913	2,829	5,254	6,130	8,178	8,178	6,130	5,185	1,495	3,937	299	757	50,285
6 Variable Costs	1,137	1,687	3,128	3,645	4,848	4,848	3,645	3,090	895	2,287	179	454	29,843
7 GROSS PROFIT	776	1,142	2,126	2,485	3,330	3,330	2,485	2,095	600	1,650	120	303	20,442
Overheads:													
8 Rent & Rates	750	750	750	750	750	750	750	750	750	750	750	750	9,000
9 Insurance	50	50	50	50	50	50	50	50	50	50	50	50	600
10 Postage & Packing	0	0	0	0	0	0	0	0	0	0	0	0	0
11 Road Tax	0	0	0	0	0	0	0	0	0	0	0	0	0
12 Vehicle Costs	0	0	0	0	0	0	0	0	0	0	0	0	0
13 Advertising	120	120	120	120	120	120	120	120	120	120	120	120	1,440
14 Stationery	10	10	10	10	10	10	10	10	10	10	10	10	120
15 Signage / Shopfront	600	0	0	0	0	0	0	0	0	0	0	0	600
16 Website	900	30	30	30	30	30	30	30	30	30	30	30	1,230
17 Telephone / Broadband	45	45	45	45	45	45	45	45	45	45	45	45	540
18 Repairs & Renewals	0	0	0	0	0	0	0	0	0	0	0	0	0
19 Heat & Light (averaged out)	85	85	85	85	85	85	85	85	85	85	85	85	1,020
20 Sundries	50	50	50	50	50	50	50	50	50	50	50	50	600
21 Professional Fees (Accountant)	650	0	0	0	0	0	0	0	0	0	0	0	650
23 Total Overheads	3,260	1,140	1,140	1,140	1,140	1,140	1,140	1,140	1,140	1,140	1,140	1,140	15,800
24 NET PROFIT	-2,484	2	986	1,345	2,190	2,190	1,345	955	-540	510	-1,020	-837	4,642
25 Own Drawings	1,200	1,200	1,200	1,200	1,200	1,200	1,200	1,200	1,200	1,200	1,200	1,200	14,400
26 Own NIC (Minimum)	12	12	12	12	12	12	12	12	12	12	12	12	144
INCOMING CAPITAL													
27 Capital Introduced	30,000												30,000
28 Loans	30,000												30,000
29													0
OUTGOING CAPITAL													
30 Initial Stock	0												0
31 Capital Purchases	0												0
32 Loan Repayments (6%, 5 yrs)	0	900	900	900	900	900	900	900	900	900	900	900	9,900
33 NET CASHFLOW	56,304	-2,110	-1,126	-767	78	78	-767	-1,157	-2,652	-1,602	-3,132	-2,949	40,198
34 Opening Bank Balance	0	56,304	54,194	53,068	52,301	52,379	52,457	51,690	50,533	47,881	46,279	43,147	0
35 Closing Bank Balance	56,304	54,194	53,068	52,301	52,379	52,457	51,690	50,533	47,881	46,279	43,147	40,198	40,198

Conclusion

Now that you have completed your Business Planning Workbook, your journey has really begun.

You should have a foundation of the steps required, and an action plan to get you on the right track to become self-employed, or to start up a small business.

The following pages contain further information, which you may find useful as your journey progresses.

The best of success with your venture.

Legislation, Regulatory Requirements and Codes of Practice which affects most businesses

General legislation:

Data Protection Act 1998 General Data Protection Regulation (GDPR) 2018

Equality Act 2010

Human Rights Act 1998

National Living Wage (Amendment) Regulations 2017

Health and Safety at Work Act 1974

The Health and Safety at Work etc. Act 1974 (General Duties of Self-Employed Persons) (Prescribed Undertakings) Regulations 2015

Copyright Designs and Patents Act 1988

Bribery Act 2010 - preventing bribery in your business and rejecting bribes from third parties

Counter Terrorism and Security Act 2015 - the Prevent strategy

Sector specific legislation and codes of practice:

Control of Substances Hazardous to Health (COSHH) Regulations 2002 - regulations for working with hazardous material

Food Hygiene Regulations 2006 - apply to aspects of farming, manufacturing, distributing and retailing food

Reporting of Injury, Disease, and Dangerous Occurrences (RIDDOR) Regulations 2013 - requirement to report serious incidents to the HSE

Health and Safety (Display Screen Equipment) Regulations 1992 - applies to people working with computer screens, etc.

Manual Handling Operations Regulations 1992 - apply to employers (i.e. by providing training) and employees (i.e. taking heed of training given by employer)

Management of Health and Safety at Work Regulations 1999

Useful Websites:

The following is a list of websites which you may find useful.

Health and Safety Executive - HSE.gov.uk

Information Commissioners Office - ICO.org.uk

ACAS (Advisory, Conciliation and Arbitration Service) - ACAS.org.uk

Equality and Human Rights Commission - EqualityHumanRights.com

Support for young entrepreneurs aged 16-30 - Shell-Livewire.org

Federation of Small Business - FSB.org.uk

Chambers of Commerce - BritishChambers.org.uk

Intellectual Property - IPO.gov.uk

The Pensions Regulator - ThePensionsRegulator.gov.uk

Companies House - CompaniesHouse.gov.uk

Charity Commission - CharityCommission.gov.uk

HMRC (The tax people) - HMRC.gov.uk

Training for Employment (Yorkshire) C.I.C. is not responsible for the content of external websites. If in doubt, please seek the advice of an independent professional.

www.ingramcontent.com/pod-product-compliance
Lightning Source LLC
Chambersburg PA
CBHW041319180526
45172CB00004B/1161